I Was a Limbo Dancer for the FBI

I Was a Limbo Dancer for the FBI

and other outrageous claims, notions, and observations

Thomas Brennan

REGENT PRESS
Berkeley, California

Copyright © 2020 by Thomas Brennan

ISBN 13: 978-1-58790-539-1

ISBN 10: 1-58790-539-6

Library of Congress Catalog Number: 2020945649

MANUFACTURED IN THE U.S.A.
REGENT PRESS
Berkeley, California
www.regentpress.net

Preface

As you're probably aware of by now, this book has nothing to do with limbo dancers or the FBI. For that I profusely apologize. What you will discover in this book, however, are my own personal notions, revelations, observations, opinions, assumptions, conclusions, judgments, inferences, suppositions, viewpoints, and impressions of whatever is happening in the world.

From time to time we have all noticed strange peculiarities as we make our way through life. My guess is that some of the observations and opinions in this book are ones shared by many of you. After all, people are basically the same everywhere. So, sit back, relax and enjoy the journey.

Am I the only one who thinks a York Peppermint Pattie is really a giant breath mint?

Anytime a movie involves a cabin – it never ends well.

I'm not sure why hotel rooms include a copy of the Gideon Bible. All I know is when I stagger back to my room after a wild night of mirth and merriment, the last thing I want to do is read a

passage from a Letter to the Corinthians.

My friend cries every time he bumps into his ex-wife. He thinks it's the mace.

Somebody out there has the worst job in the world – and he's *still* showing up on Monday.

It's strange how every November, Americans eat food that comes out of a bird's butt.

My therapist is beginning to annoy me. At my last session she told me I'm obsessed with food. I laughed so hard I almost dropped my lasagna.

It's odd how the words give *up*, give *out*, and give *in* mean the same thing.

Remember when your mother warned you to always wear clean underwear in case you ended up in the emergency room? If you end up in the ER, I think clean underwear is

going to be the last thing on your mind.

I understand Walmart now offers flu shots. I'm a little leery about that.
I don't want somebody sticking me with a needle and then a minute later they're stocking produce.

When somebody says, "I owe you an apology," don't they *still* owe you an apology?

I hate sitting through really old movies where it takes somebody a half hour just to dial a number.

You know you're too fat if your bathroom scale has a restraining order against you.

If psychics are so good at predicting the future, how come they never expect you?

You know you're turning into your parents if you add water to ketchup to make it last longer.

Awkward moment: When I'm the only one in the audience clapping, thinking the performance is over – and it's not.

I like to keep things simple. My 6th grade science project was a can of lighter fluid and a match.

Graduating from college doesn't guarantee you gainful employment any more than a beard and a plaid shirt makes you a lumberjack.

My first apartment was so small – I could cook from my bed.

I don't understand the message behind the Boston Tea Party. Angry patriots dressed like NATIVE AMERICANS protesting England's tax on WHITE colonists.

How much time should go by before you throw away a birthday card from your mother?

I'm not in the best shape. I get winded taking a nap.

You know your vital signs are horrible if your doctor gives you the name of a good coroner.

You know you're REALLY old if you remember the Big Bang.

The Jawbreaker – It's the only candy honest enough to warn you of an impending health hazard. I find that commendable.

I hate it when somebody says, "That's funny!" and they don't laugh.

I made the mistake of visiting North Dakota in the winter. That was 6 years ago. My left foot still hasn't thawed out.

My cat is very finicky about what she eats. My question is this. For an animal that enjoys licking its butt, how can ANYTHING taste bad?

I don't know why people say they work *out* of their house when in fact they work *in* their house.

What's up with Santa Claus and the Tooth Fairy? Complete strangers breaking into homes while everyone's asleep. That's supposed to be acceptable behavior? What kind of

sick, delusional fantasies are we teaching our kids?

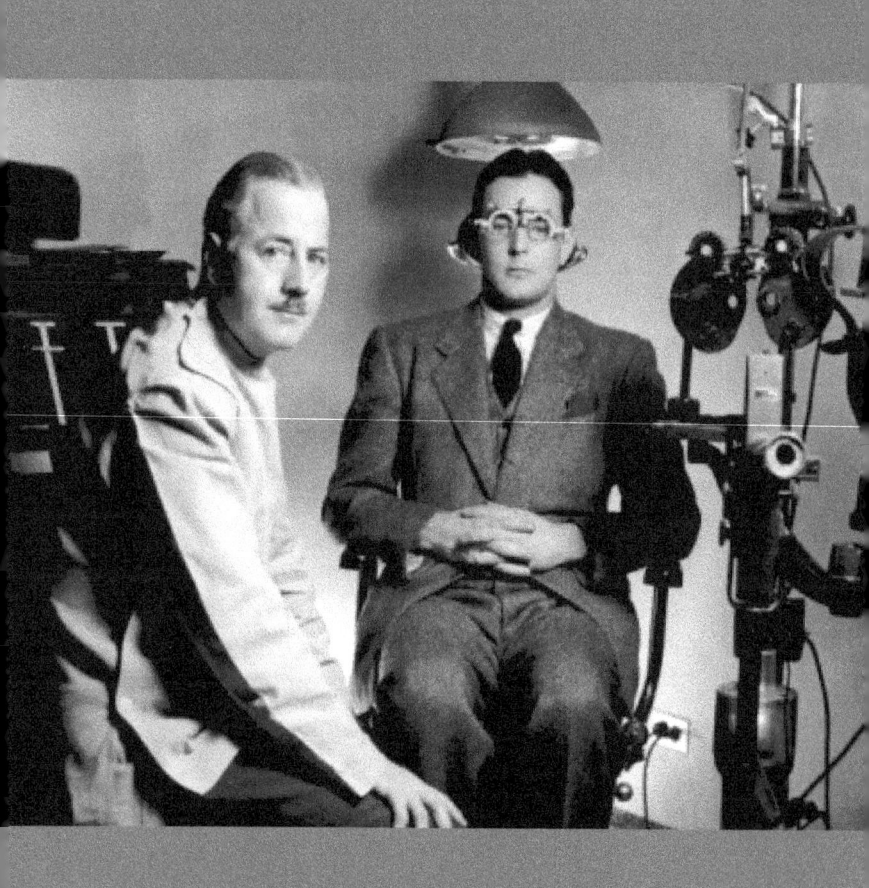

I had an argument with my doctor. He insisted on taking my temperature rectally. Now I have to find another optometrist.

I had a horrible nightmare recently. I dreamed I shared a hot tub with a couple of Victoria's Secret models — and I was Eleanor Roosevelt.

Ever get caught talking to yourself? So that nobody thinks I'm crazy, I just tell them I'm answering the voices in my head.

I went to a school that was so mean, the *teachers* stole my lunch money.

I've been in the dumps lately. The other day my wife said to me, "What's wrong, honey? You look terrible. Why don't you pull the gun out of your mouth so we can talk?"

They say the best revenge is to live well. The trouble with that advice is it takes too much effort.

The summers are definitely getting warmer. One day it was so unbearable, I sat in a hot tub just to cool off.

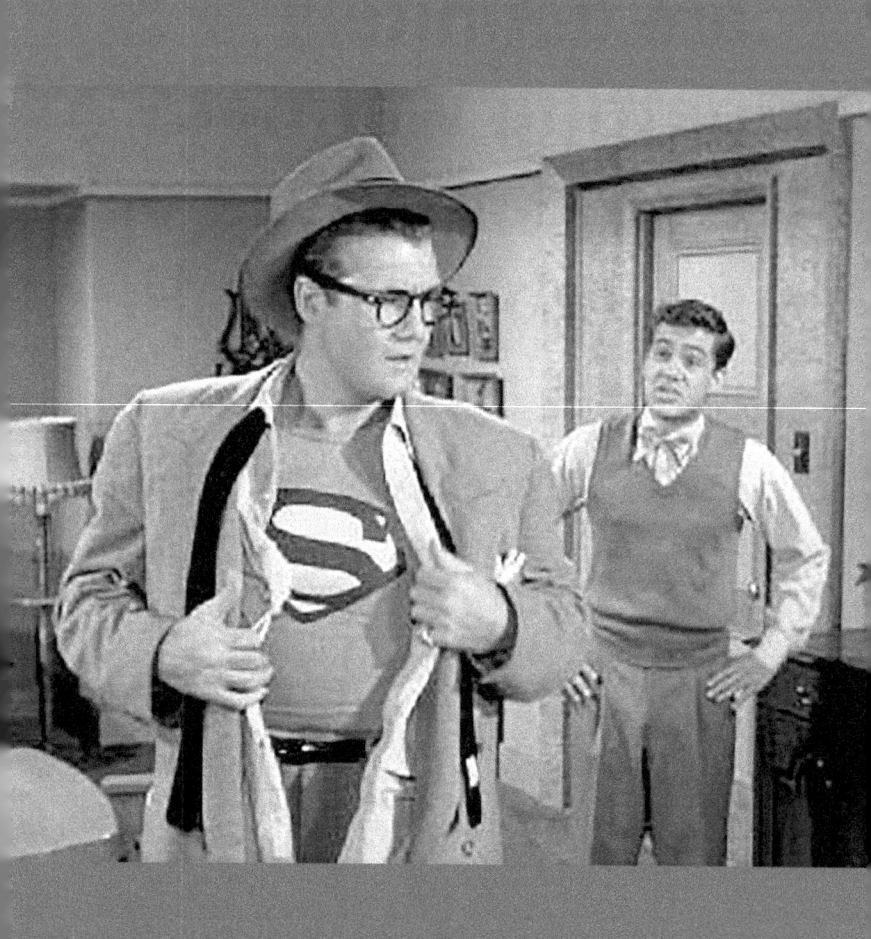

It's amazing how easily Superman gets away with pretending he's Clark Kent. How observant can the reporters at the Daily Planet be if they can't even recognize Superman through a pair of fake eye glasses?

If somebody talks *behind* your back, aren't they really talking in *front* of your back?

I like making
new friends.
But then again,
I like acid reflux.

The St. Valentine's Day Massacre. It's a stark reminder of how violent our history is. It should tell you something when *St. Valentine's Day* and *Massacre* are in the same sentence.

Standup comics and hardened criminals have a lot in common. Many of them are introverted, they travel a lot, often work alone, and they both like to kill their audience.

Bill Gates is so rich – God mows his lawn.

I'm not afraid of flying.
I just don't want my flight to be made into a movie.

You know how you exaggerate to impress someone so they'll go out with you?
I had to convince this one date that I don't look the same today as I do on the nickel.

Have you noticed the more lost you are, the faster you drive?

I had a really bad day today. I got beat up at a Friendly's.

I enjoy flying. But I get nervous sitting in an emergency exit seat. The flight crew expects you to help passengers in the event of a crash. Apparently, the only qualification you need for saving lives is that you purchased an airline ticket.

Have you ever suddenly lost your balance while standing in line and then you pretend your awkwardness was intended?

Cuddling is a very enjoyable experience. Especially when you're with someone.

I can't believe the people chosen for jury duty are allowed to determine someone else's fate. Half of them look like they're one step away from being an inmate.

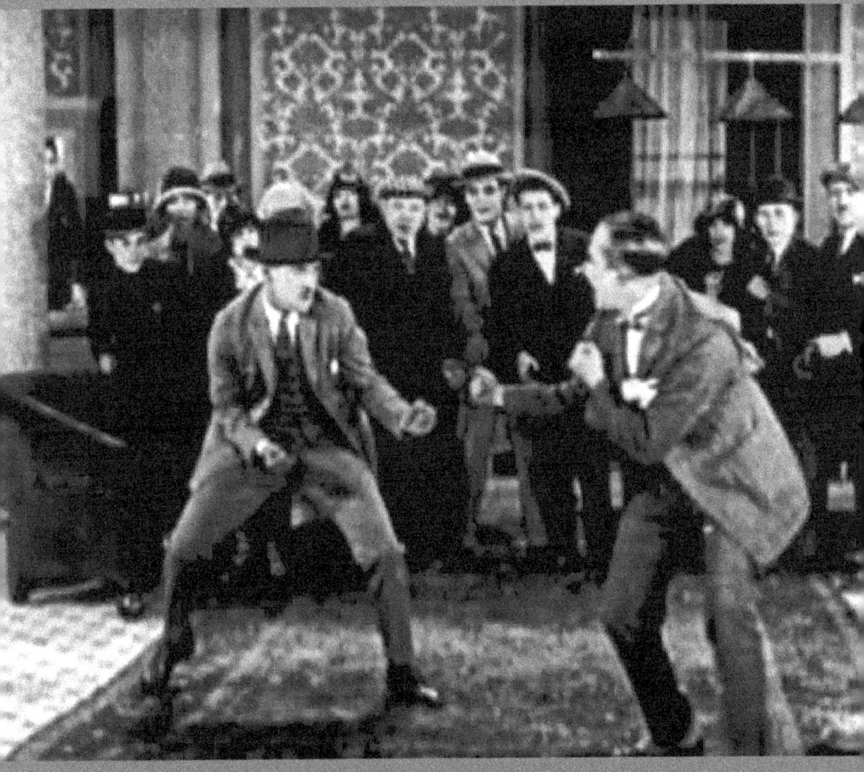

You know you're turning into your dad if you start poking holes in your belt.

I come from a rough part of town. Just to give you an idea how rough, the priest in my neighborhood moonlighted as a hitman.

I have a serious pet peeve.
I hate hearing people's knees crack when they squat.

I think owning a gun is a little like owning a toilet plunger. People might want to keep one around the house, but they never want to have to use it.

I hate sushi. I don't enjoy eating anything that looks like it belongs on the end of a hook.

Texans are tough. I went to this one bar. They didn't have a mechanical bull. You had to ride a real one.

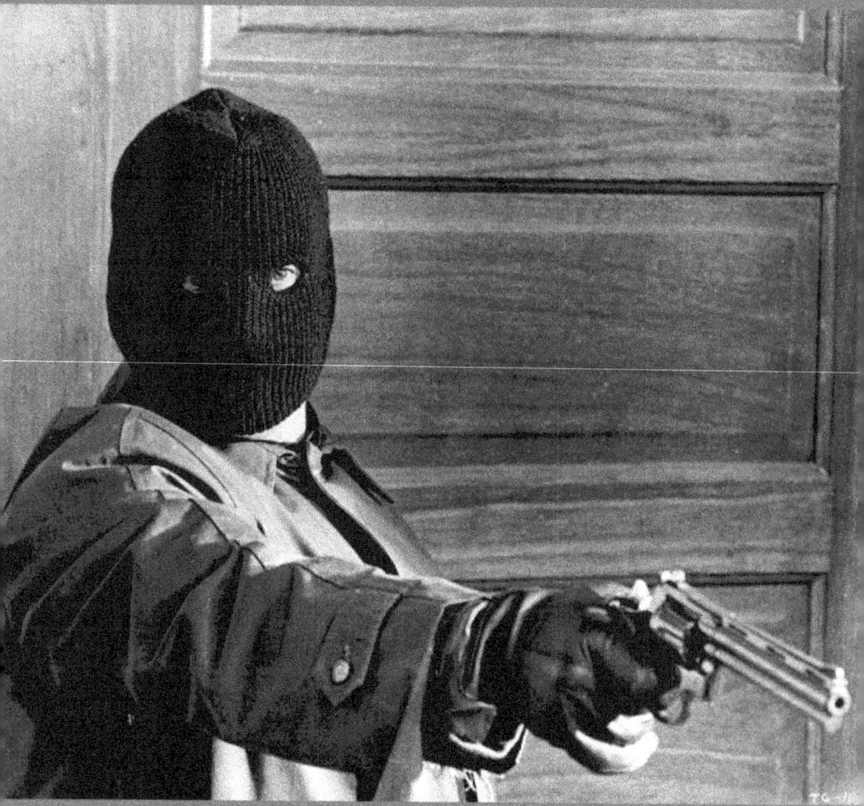

I don't trust anybody on Craig's List. You don't know anything about these people. And they certainly shouldn't be allowed inside your home – unless you want to end up as patio furniture.

You might have a drinking problem if bartenders tell you they need to close up.

I think it's ludicrous for professional baseball players to pray for a hit. God's not concerned about which team drives in the winning run. The Creator has more pressing matters to deal with – Like famine – devastating diseases – the Kardashians.

You probably don't have a good medical plan if your doctor uses a tip jar.

The drug situation in this country is getting out of hand. The other day I drove by a Nativity Scene and the three wisemen were freebasing.

I don't think my gym teacher liked me. He made me go out for javelin catching.

If you read a self-help book, isn't someone other than yourself helping you?

How about those commercials that claim for just $19.95 a month you can feed a family of four? Just $19.95 a month. All I want to know is how can I get in on this?

I have no luck. Except once when I won a raffle at work. I got to spend a weekend overlooking a wet market in Wuhan.

I'm currently writing a true story about a spy hiding in plain sight in Communist Russia: *I Was Stalin's Mustache*.

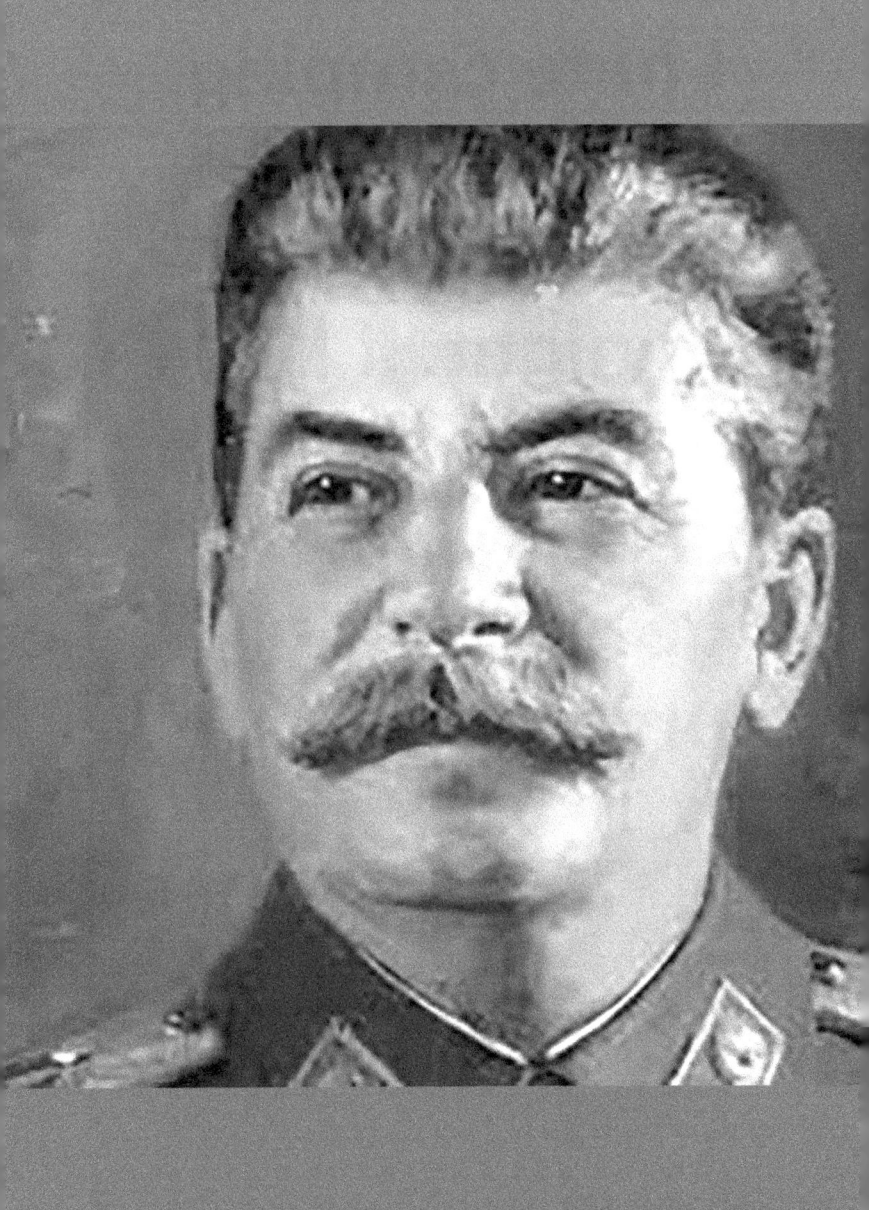

I hate camping. The woods creep me out at night. If I hear a branch snap – I've got a laundry problem.

I have to admit – I'm a little superstitious. I think if you have an itchy foot, it means a man named Julius will enter your life and then go just as quickly – leaving you with a bad cough.

When scientists determine that another species has become extinct, how do they know?

I stopped taking my medication because of the side effects. For 3 days I thought I was being followed by men with dimples.

Sportscasters earn way too much money for stating the obvious. "He swings at the ball and misses - That's a strike!" Gee – thanks for clearing that up – I never would have guessed.

I got a postcard from an ex-girlfriend recently. The front showed a picture of Forest Lawn Cemetery. On the back she wrote, "Wish you were here."

Have you noticed there's not enough songs about tainted meat?

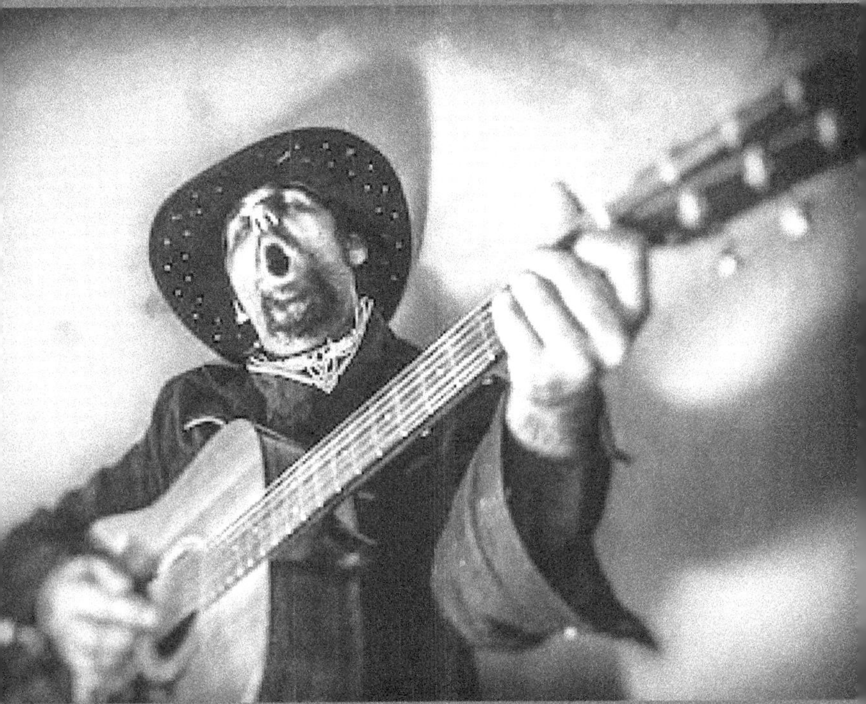

You might be a narcissist if you take a bow after sex.

I hate the expression, "There's more than one way to skin a cat." First of all, who the hell is skinning cats? And there's more than one way? I think at this point the law needs to step in.

I used to live in a town that was so strict, I was picked up for stealing a glance.

It's easy for someone to say you should "Grin and bear it." All I know is if I'm hit in the face with a claw hammer, I'm pretty sure grinning is not going to be my first reaction.

It's impossible to fall down a flight of stairs and chew gum at the same time.

I don't understand the saying, "No use crying over spilled milk!" All I know is anybody who cries over spilled milk has bigger issues than a minor kitchen accident.

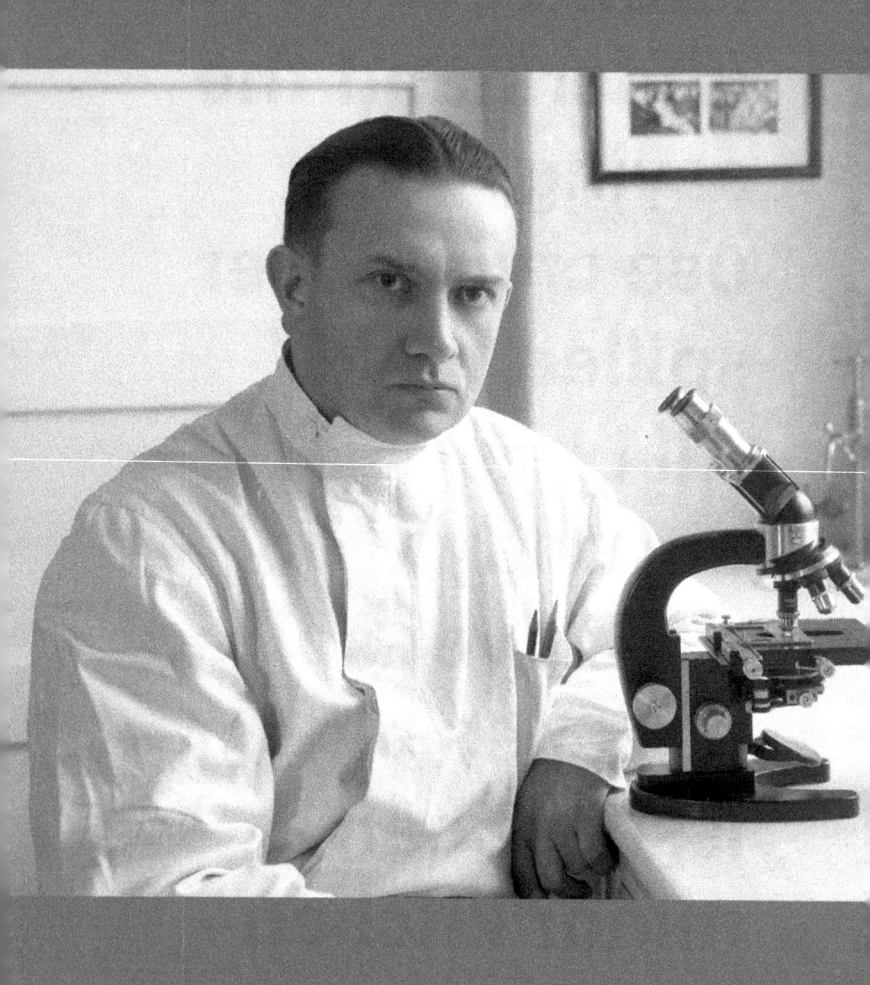

I come from a long line of dedicated researchers in the field of science. My uncle was the first to discover sarcasm in meatloaf.

Food poisoning is no laughing matter. Or as it's called at my house – dinner.

A new book I'm working on – *Attila the Hun: A Love Story.*

I don't understand the part of the song that goes, "I've been working on the railroad, just to pass the time away..." First of all, if I want to pass the time away, working on the railroad is near the bottom of

my to do list. Down there with having my chest hair ripped out by its roots.

I think I'm getting crankier as I grow older. The other day I told a librarian to lower her voice.

I hate when I turn my T–shirt inside out only to find that it was right side out to begin with.

Christmas is a strange holiday. We drag a freshly slaughtered tree into our home, decorate it with ornaments, and after we've grown tired of it, we kick it to the curb on trash day. I think if a tree could get hold of a good lawyer, it might have a pretty strong case.

Con Edison
PM FAIR.
NEAR 40°
F RAIN S/N
SNOW-COLD.
NEAR 50° THEN
PM COLDER.
20°s

Meteorologists provide way too much information about the weather. I don't care about the barometric pressure or the direction the wind is blowing or how cold it is in Balls, Montana. Just tell me how to dress.

Sometimes I fake a sneeze just to get a "Bless you!" from a complete stranger.

Why is a funeral vigil called a *wake* if the person is *dead*?

I think the Ten Commandments should be revisited. "Thou Shalt Not Kill" is number 5 on the list, yet missing the Sabbath is number 3. I just don't think skipping church is worse than burying a body in the back yard.

Ever notice when you see or hear the words, "effective immediately," it's never a good thing?

I wonder if there's a white neighborhood that's so bigoted, even white people aren't welcome.

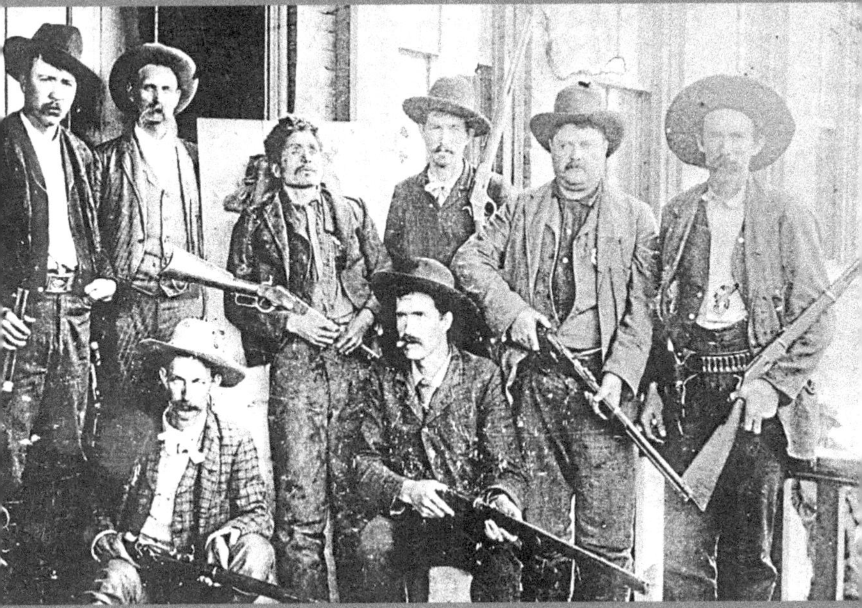

As of this writing, *Mission Impossible 6* is the latest installment in that franchise. I have one question. If the missions are so impossible, how come there are six of them?

The express line at the supermarket is a joke. There's always some cretin fighting with the cashier over coupons that expired during the Carter administration.

I told my wife I caught a man hiding in some bushes while trying to peek into our bedroom window. The next day she planted more bushes.

So many people suffer from dementia. The other night a burglar broke into my home and forgot why he was there.

I told everybody I won't eat anything with a face. My family was relieved to hear that.

How about those tiny packets of snacks flight attendants hand out? Are they serious? Actually, the snacks are just about the right size – if you're a hamster.

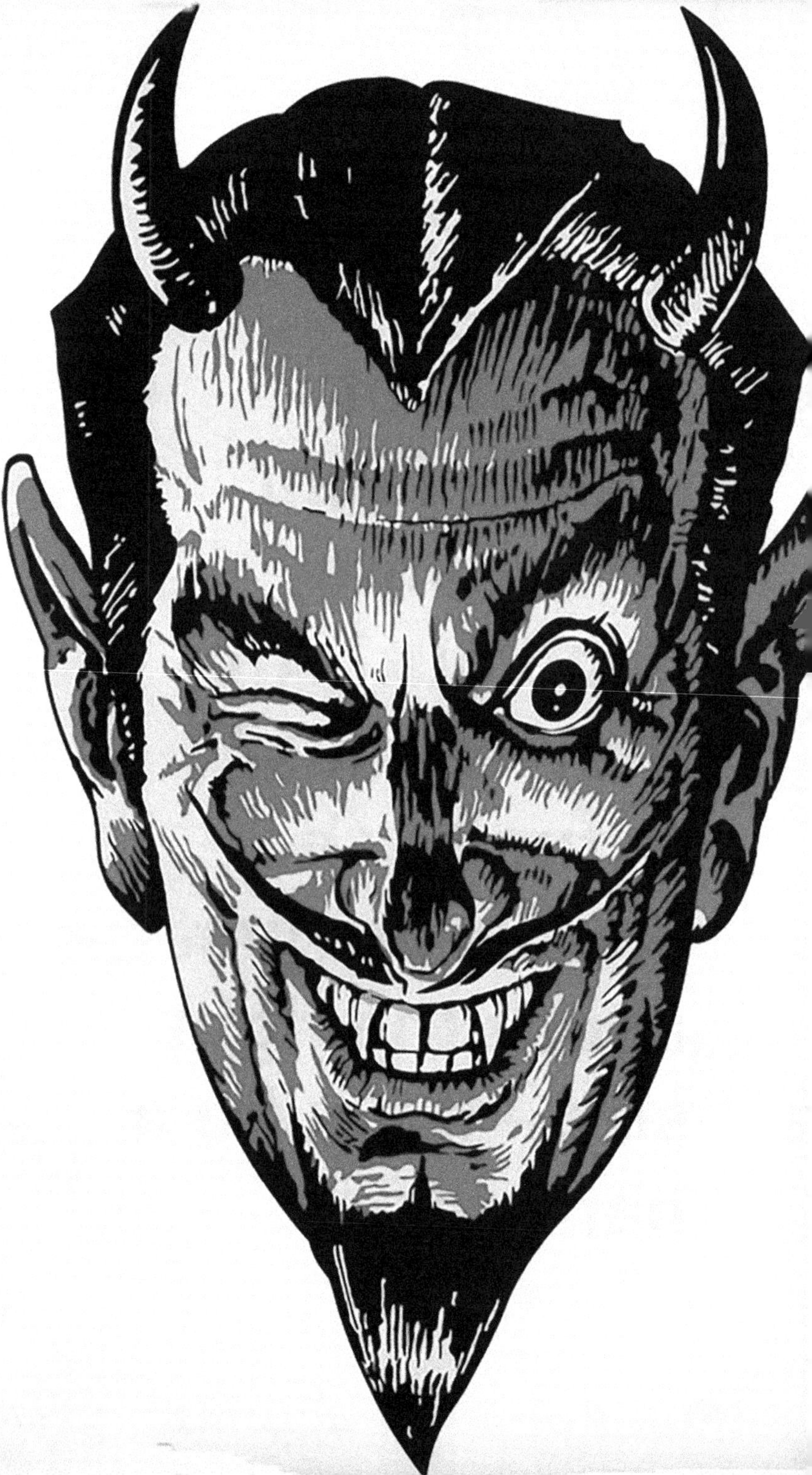

A little-known fact I want to pass along. If you attempt to play a DVD in a CD player, you can actually hear Satan.

I wasted 2 years of my life behind the counter at a convenience store. I didn't work there. I just stood behind the counter.

My mother-in-law and I never got along. One time I took her to a theme park where lions roam free. I tried to convince her it was a petting zoo.

It's been said that it is better to light a candle than to curse the darkness. Yeah – well try finding a candle in the dark.

Pets are amazing. Dogs are always happy to see you. Cats, on the other hand, look at you as if to say, "You still here?"

I worry about my friend. He thinks a coat of arms is something Jeffrey Dahmer wore.

I don't have a good nose for business. I once invested my life's savings in a company that claimed it could turn nuclear waste into an after-dinner mint.

I recently joined Liars Anonymous. Or did I?

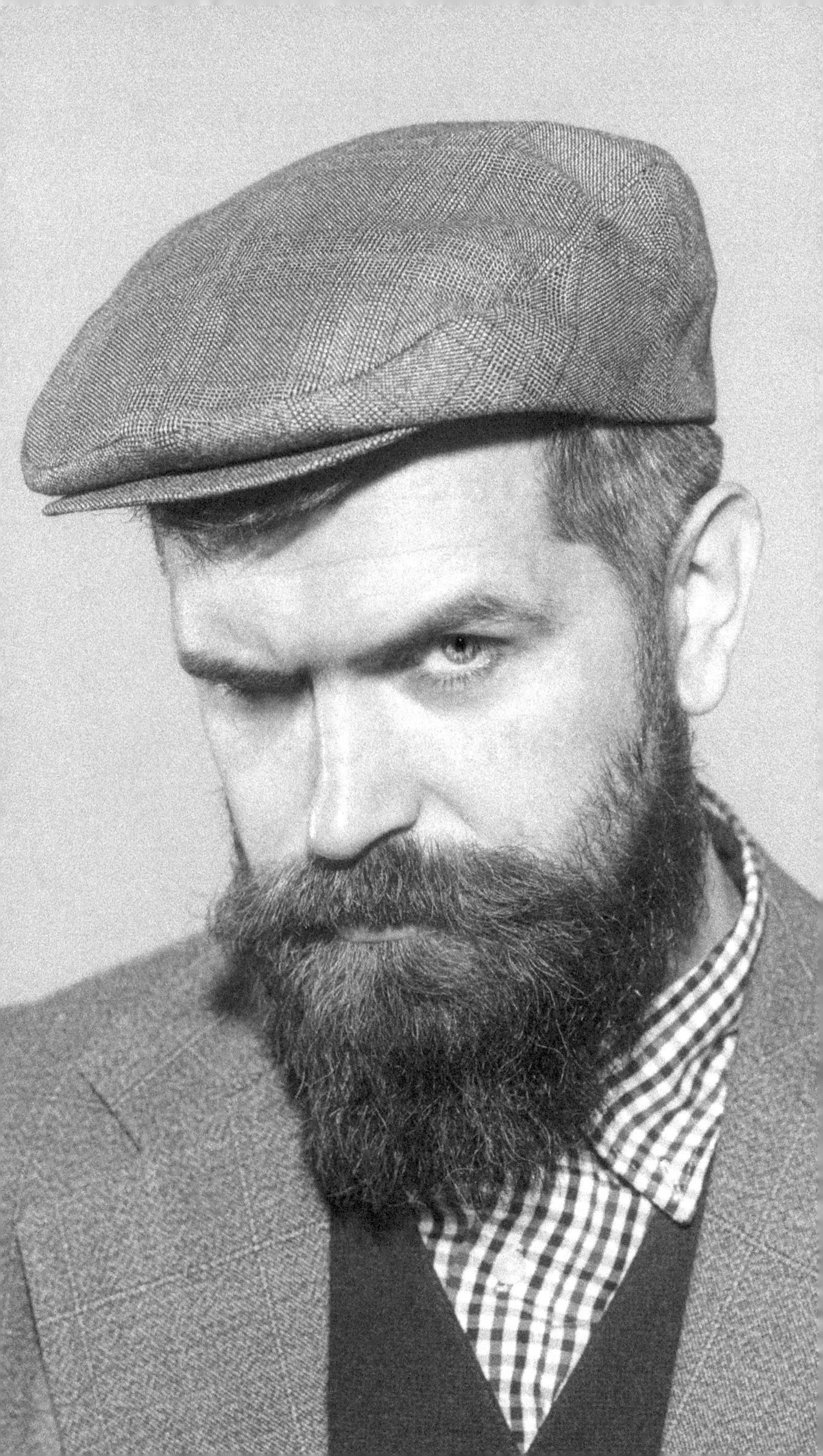

I hate hearing about people's dreams. I'd rather eat a plate of bad clams.

I love eating breakfast out. Just one problem. Why does juice come in such a tiny glass and yet they serve pancakes the size of the Cumberland Gap?

People who don't smoke and people who don't drink are frequently judged differently. If you don't smoke, people think you care about your health. If you don't drink, they suspect you're a recovering alcoholic.

I keep hearing about people trying to find Jesus. Folks – If Jesus hasn't been found after 2,000 years – He never will be.

If it wasn't for food, nobody would visit anyone.

Ever notice when somebody walks up to a bar in a movie, the bartender is ALWAYS available?

For a guy who lives in the jungle, how come Tarzan is always clean-shaven?

"I just happened to be in the neighborhood" really means, **"I'm stalking you."**

There will NEVER be a one-man play entitled, *An Evening with Ted Bundy*.

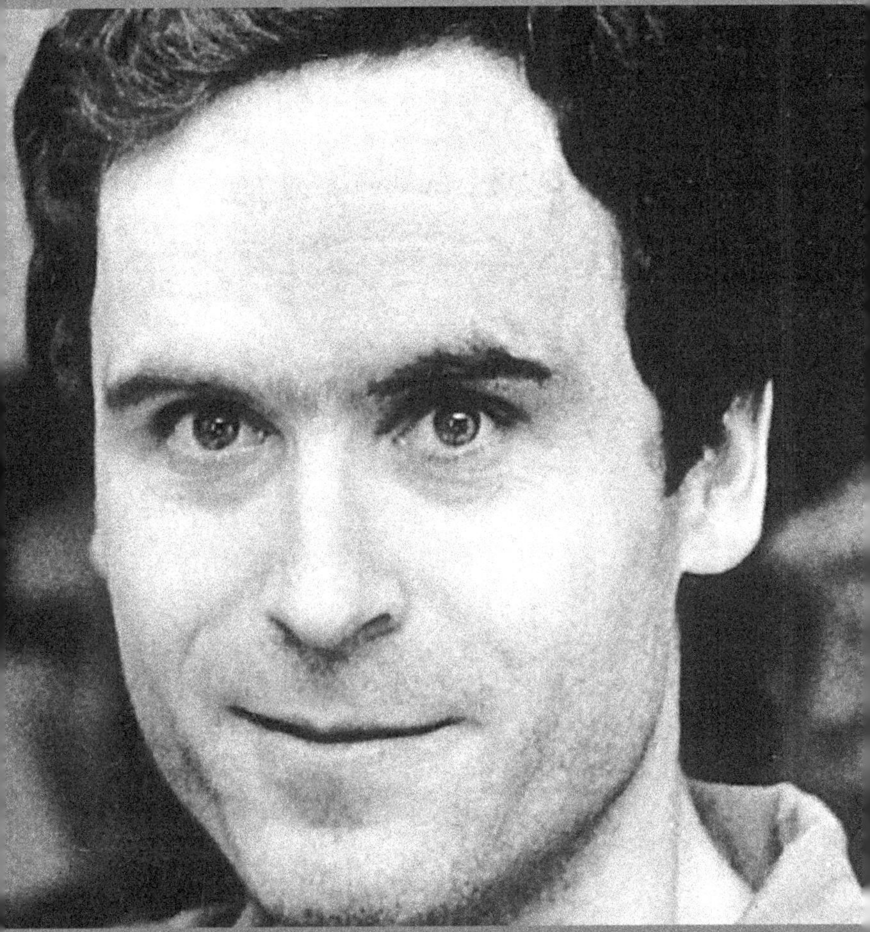

How come fans aren't allowed to talk during a golfer's swing, yet it's okay to scream at a batter facing a ball coming at him at 100 miles an hour?

Only two things get me up in the morning. Food – and Peter Falk impressions.

NOTES:

NOTES: